Lessons for Leaders

Leaders are neither "made" nor "born."

Leadership is a CHOICE that you make for yourself.

By Tod Faller

Happiness and Misery are also Choices --

Choose Wisely,

Peace,

Tod Faller

Lessons For Leaders

By
Tod Faller

To order additional copies of this book or for book publishing information, or to contact the author:

Headline Books & Co., P.O. Box 52, Terra Alta, WV 26764
www.headlinebooks.com

Tel/Fax: 800-570-5951 or 304-789-3001
Email: tod@todfaller.com
www.todfaller.com

ISBN 9780929915418

Library of Congress Control Number: 2006924800

PRINTED IN THE UNITED STATES OF AMERICA

DEDICATION

...To You:

Each time you choose
to persevere when all appears lost;

Each time you choose happiness
over despair;

Each time you try again...
when giving up would be easier;

Each time you choose to
rise above rejection;

Each time you choose to love
and allow yourself *to be* loved;

Each time you love, accept, forgive
and *choose* to be happy.

...for my grandbabies

Contents

FORWARD

"I never liked Jazz Music. But I was outside the Bagdad Theater in Portland one night when I saw a man playing the saxophone. I stood there for fifteen minutes, and he never opened his eyes. After that I liked Jazz.

Sometime you have to watch somebody love something before you can love it yourself. It is as if they are showing you the way."

— Donald Miller, *Blue Like Jazz*

INTRODUCTION

Leaders are those who understand human behavior, accept human differences and choose to be a catalyst for constructive change and organizational growth.

If we lived it, a memory was born and subsequently stored in the data base of the mind. When evoked, these memories are available for instant recall. Words, pictures, touch, sounds, even aromas are stimuli that can automatically pull these memories from those experiences in the same way a computer pulls images from your hard drive to the monitor. Events, music, places, words and phrases are enough stimuli to rekindle those memories.

Words on the written page are nothing more than the labels we give to our memories; the mental pictures in our mind. Books are full of "labels" that serve to stir those memories and pull those pictures to the surface. New pictures are developed with each new experience. To awaken the memories of those who would lead, what follows is a collection of independent thoughts and phrases in *The Teacher Down the Hall Seminar Series.*

As no two people will have exactly the same experiences, no two of us will relate in exactly the same way to the people, images or objects in our lives. As a result, the same words or phrases that may impact one person, may not carry the same weight, significance or relevance for another. What follows, however, will be something that *will* speak to everyone...guaranteed!

May the following pages stir positive memories within *you.* May these passages inspire you to rekindle lost relationships, awaken hope, and remind you that leadership is *truly*...a choice that you make for yourself.

To whom much is given...

Business or industry, ministry or counseling, education or politics, sales or service, leadership in every organization has at least one thing in common. We are ALL subject to the First Rule of Leadership.

The First Rule is the guiding principle of leadership. It needs to be framed and placed on the desk of every individual charged with the responsibility for serving others. Center it at the top of every memo; engraved it above every doorway, make it the preamble to every contract, and the mantra at every team meeting.

The First Rule is as old as Christianity itself. It applies to all who serve. It is not philosophical, nor is it vague. It is not intended to be a gentle reminder. Those who serve as leaders, live by it. It is your obligation; it is the First Rule of Leadership:

"To whom much is given, much will be asked"

The WELL

Imagine being in the bottom of a deep, dark, cold well. You scream and cry for help, but there is no one to hear you. The longer you remain in that well, the more your fears deepen as loneliness and despair grip you like a vise. The absolute isolation becomes harder and harder to accept. Your mind wanders, your thoughts become distorted, your stomach is in knots, your head and body ache, and your screams, for all practical purposes, might as well be shouted in complete silence.

Then, suddenly, you hear a voice. Your cries for help have been heard. From the top of the well comes the invitation you have been waiting so long to hear: *"I'm here to help you."*

Someone is offering you a lifeline. In that moment, you experience an explosion of joy as you realize that your safety, your happiness, your life itself is being handed to you by this person. You want to know, *"Who's out there?"* Is it...a counselor, a friend, a family member, a co-worker, a stranger? Does it really matter? No one *put* you in this well, you jumped into it entirely on your own. Regardless of why you went in, you know now that you want out. You have your hand on the lifeline. Only **you** can decide to begin the journey out. You need only to step beyond your pride to begin the climb.

Each of us must choose for ourselves:
to remain within the well. . . or to begin the climb out.

You *can not* change what you *will not* acknowledge.

There are billions of people on this planet; each individual being distinctive and unique. Often, our differences are abundantly obvious. In fact, we seem to readily accept that visual barriers such as cultural, religious, ethnic, language, status and/or our environmental differences will breed conflict. Intellectually, we know these are not *reasons* for people to choose conflict, but our experiences have convinced us to acknowledge that conflict will flourish around such differences.

We all come from different worlds of experiences. Because of these differences, everyone carries his/her own unique gifts and talents into a relationship. When I can share my strengths with you, and you are willing to offer me your strengths where I am weak, we both become stronger than we could have become on our own. Yet we live in conflict because we continue to believe that life is, *"All about me."*

Our conflicts arise not *because* we are different from each other, but because we fail to *accept* that we are different. We want people to accept *us*, to give *us* what we want when we want it, to understand our moods, to listen to us, to affirm us, and to tend to our every need. Our interpersonal conflicts rage not because "*I am different from you*" but because "*You are different from me.*" Our conflicts will not diminish as long as we continue to believe that we have no responsibility for the welfare and justice of those around us; as long as we insist that life is *"All about Me."*

change (con't.)

So what is it I am refusing to accept? What is at the root of my frequent bouts of anger, frustrations, impatience, jealousy, selfishness and hate when others won't do or say whatever *I* think they "should" say or "ought to" do? Why is it I continue to shout, *"You just don't get it!"* when my feelings, pride or dignity are shattered by the actions of others?

Of all our human differences, each individual's peace of mind remains elusive because of this simple truth: We will not acknowledge...nor accept that each of us has the free will to make creative, responsible and independent choices for ourselves. Within each of us, our human needs are screaming, *"I need to be loved and accepted; I am important; I deserve equality and demand respect. I must be free to choose for myself. I want **you** to notice **me**!. I WANT WHAT I WANT WHEN I WANT IT!"*

We want others to change, but the fact remains:
You can *not* change in others
what you will *not* acknowledge...nor accept, in yourself.

All of Life is Awareness

It is easier to blame, than to accept ownership for our actions. It is easier to find fault, than to find solutions. It is easier to hide from the truth, than to acknowledge it.

Carl Rodgers, the father of Rodgerian Counseling, believed that all of the answers to life's questions were *"already within us. We have but to uncover them."*

David Carradean played the lead in the now decades old "Kung Fu" television series. While attempting to find enlightenment among the monks in the shau-lin temple, he would persistently stumble in his quest to find inner peace. Time and time again, the old Kung Fu master would center him with one word: *"Focus."*

My spiritual director in the seminary often challenged me. She delighted in reminding me to dig from within to find the *"Peace that was within me."* Instead of telling me to "focus," her word was "Awareness." Time and time again, instead of answering my questions, she would only come back with, "All *of life is Awareness. Accept what is yours."*

It has taken decades for this to sink in.
Accept what is yours.

Peace on Earth

Some spend hours, literally hours, picking out just the right card to send just the right message to loved ones on those special occasions. At Christmas, you buy cards by the box. What attracted you to this particular box of cards? Inspirational passage? Pretty picture? On sale? What message were you sending?

If, for example, you sent Christmas cards last year, that said, "Peace on Earth," how many appeals did you really make for Peace on Earth? Each time you signed your name were you acknowledging some effort on your part to actually *bring about* peace this year? With each new card, were you pledging to make a difference in the life of that particular individual or family? With each fresh signature, were you acknowledging that peace doesn't have a chance *"without ME?"* Or with each card were you simply one card closer to checking this annual obligation off your list?

What are *you* doing to bring about peace?

The truth is, if you want *peace* in your organization,
you must work for peace.
To have peace, you must work for Justice.

Inner Strength: Inner Peace

A man was walking in the woods and came upon a bear. Frightened, the man backpedaled, tripped over a log, fell over the hill, and broke his leg. As he lay there, unable to get up, he saw the bear come to the top of the hill and look down at him. The man mustered his strength, and began to pray. "Lord, please save me. I need a miracle here, Lord. I need… I need… I need you to make that bear a Christian!"

And just like that… the man witnessed a miracle. Immediately the bear stopped in his tracks, got down on his knees, put his paws together and looked to the heavens. Suddenly he heard the bear say, *"Thank you, Lord, for the meal I am about to receive!"*

The message might be, be careful what you pray for! But the question is, where do Leaders find their strength?

As a Leader, your strength is in your people… your colleagues. Their gifts to the solutions you seek are all around you; you have only to be *aware* of what surrounds you. Are you making conscious decisions, or do your habits have you on cruise control? Find a catch phrase. Refer to it as your anchor. A simple catch phrase like *"Accept what is yours"* is just a reminder to be conscious of life, to observe, to focus, to be centered. That knot in your stomach is telling you something. Are you listening to it? You recognize the times when the voice from within was leading you to do what you knew was the *right thing to do*…did you heed that voice? When you believe the next decision will lead you to a place of peace… will you follow it?

Leaders listen to those they serve… then trust in themselves to lead.

Perception is Reality

Because we disagree, it doesn't mean that either of us "lied."

Everyone operates out of his/her own perception of truth...out of his/her own world of experience. Understanding is not possible without experience.

In the absence of understanding, we speculate; we fill the void with our *perception* of what happened...our perception becomes our "truth."

What actually happened, therefore, will vary dramatically and in direction proportion to the number of witnesses present.

Perception isn't really reality.
But if people believe in the perception, it will define their reality.

We just gotta Know

Speculation will diminish in direct proportion to Understanding

We watch magicians make tigers appear in an empty cage, we are amazed to see airplanes disappear in front of our eyes, and we hold our breath each time the pretty lady gets sawed in half. We want to know *"How did he do that?"* Everyone has a theory. Everyone simply wants to understand.

In recent years, however, the "Masked Magician" has been doing his best to reveal how these illusions are being performed. He has taken the mystery out of some of the magic tricks that have been keeping audiences on the edges of their seats forever. Consequently, we no longer have to speculate how the lady gets sawed in half. We now know the trick. Now that we really do understand, we don't have to guess anymore. In fact, when we truly understood, our appetite "to know" was appeased and our need for further speculation, i.e., guessing, rumors, gossip, about what we didn't understand, simply vanished.

Avoid speculation. . . open wide the lines of communication.

PLAY BALL !

When your child was just an infant, he/she would sit (or be propped up against the couch), and you would slowly roll the ball. You and the child would spread your legs out wide to ensure success in "catching" the ball. As time went on, and the child got a bit older, the ball could be rolled a little faster, and his/her ability to roll it back would be more controlled and accurate as it came back to you. When the child could coordinate his/her hands to actually hold and catch the ball, you didn't need to roll it anymore. You tossed it in a slow, underhand way. You made sure the child was prepared for the ball, saying "ready?" and then gently making the toss. When the child caught the ball, you praised the child, clapped your hands, and invited other adults to watch how splendidly the child "played ball."

As the months passed, the child grew to become more proficient in the game. He/she learned to catch the ball more often and to better control the accuracy of the throw. You could throw overhand, but still not too hard. With more practice, of course, the speed of the ball was increased. A natural trust was established that neither would throw the ball more forcefully than the other was prepared to receive. If one occasionally dropped the ball, it would be deemed an acceptable action as the occasional mistake or periods of inattention would be viewed as both natural and unintentional.

True Communication is *exactly* like this. To establish a relationship with another, you must first take a chance...and start by "rolling the ball" in his/her direction. Toss gently—keep your eye on the ball—and be still when it is your turn "to catch." A dropped ball would then not be grounds for either party to suddenly stop playing the game and stomp away.

And neither party would expect the other to suddenly feel compelled to begin pitching the ball directly at the other's head! We only do that in the *absence* of communications.

Developing STRUCTURE...setting BOUNDARIES

1. *You* must first establish the *boundaries.* (E.G .CLASSROOM RULES: PROCEDURES AND ROUTINES)

2. *YOU* MUST THEN TEACH THE *BOUNDARIES.* (NOT JUST *TELL*...BUT *TEACH* THE BEHAVIORS YOU NOW EXPECT.)

3. *YOU* MUST CLEARLY DEFINE THE *CONSEQUENCES* FOR STAYING WITHIN...AND STEPPING OUTSIDE OF... THESE *BOUNDARIES.* (REWARDS AND PENALTIES) OTHERS *WILL NOW CHOOSE* THEIR OWN *BEHAVIORS.* (LIKE IT OR NOT...)

4. OTHERS MUST NOW CONSISTENTLY RECEIVE (FROM *YOU*) THE PROMISED, EARNED, AND ANTICIPATED CONSEQUENCES FOR THE BEHAVIOR CHOICES *THEY* MAKE. (REWARDS AND PENALTIES)

IF *YOU DO NOT* PROVIDE THE PROMISED, EARNED, AND ANTICIPATED CONSEQUENCES,

THEN, *WHO* MOVED THE *BOUNDARIES*?

The FOUR "A's" of Active Listening

ATTITUDE: Adapt the attitude that this is our conversation, not mine or yours. Take the pledge: *"I will focus on the listener to avoid stealing the focus."*

ACKNOWLEDGE: Let the speaker see that he/she has been *heard*.

AIM Your Posture: Speakers must believe that you care about them; about what they have to say. Your body language sends nonverbal messages much louder than any words you speak.

AYE (eye) Contact: Make this connection with your listener. The eyes are referred to as the gateway to the soul and are the most valued Interpersonal communication asset you possess.

Hearing is NOT listening.
Become proficient at active listening and you will find others treating you differently, more positively, and they won't even know why they're doing it—Guaranteed!*

* See Seminars in the back of this book.

Sorry, you just THINK..."It's all about ME."

Understanding is critical to open communications. We cognitively accept the premise... but only as long as *others* are first willing to accept *us!* We think every conversation, every opportunity to relate with others, every comment spoken within earshot, every glance in our direction, every word or inference... is *"all about me."*

We guard against revealing "too much" for fear that we might be judged by what we say (in the same way we judge others by what they say and even how they say it). In this way, the opportunity to enhance understanding is often shortchanged. We tend to read *our own* experiences and perceptions into everything we hear from others. We plan our responses even before the one speaking has finished their sentence. We grow impatient with others. We grow weary of tolerating those around us. Why don't they understand? "Don't you people get it! I just want *you,* to understand *me.*"

Oddly enough, what you are hoping for... the "understanding of me," is exactly what the person standing across from you is hoping for, too.

Both parties in chance meetings or purposeful conversations secretly insist on being the first one to be understood, and subsequently, accepted. We exert limitless behaviors and attempts to control to get our message...our signals out there. How often do we fail to grasp the concept that we are not the only person in the conversation, relationship, negotiation, classroom, sale, family, etc., trying to send that message?

The secret is this: Work to meet the needs of others, and you will find *others* tripping over themselves to meet your needs.

Looking beyond Behaviors

Two kindergarten children were on the playground when the little girl said to the little boy, "Let's play house."
"How do you do that?"
"The best I can figure out," she explained, "is one of us has to communicate."
"What does that mean?" The boy asked.
"You don't know? Great! You can be the husband!"

To understand your interpersonal conflicts, the key is to understand both *how and why* we humans communicate and behave the way we do. Understanding comes in discovering how our differing perceptions, experiences, and human Needs *so completely* dictate our behaviors and impact our personal relationships. We communicate our wants and needs through these filters. *Every* behavior is motivated by the intent to meet one (or more) of our basic human needs.

We dedicate far too much energy *reacting* to the unwanted or unwelcome behaviors that spark misunderstandings and far too little energy *responding* to the source...the motivation...that lies behind the behaviors.

Conflict Resolution is all about learning to look *past* unwanted, inappropriate, or negative behaviors to meet the need that spawned those behaviors.*

*See Seminars in the back of this book.

EXCUSE me?

A school teacher can never take the safety of his/her children for granted. He/she is always on guard for their safety.

I was on morning duty, waiting for the last of the "drop offs" to make their way out of their parent's car and scurry across the playground and into the school cafeteria to begin another school day. This was Monday morning after the extended Thanksgiving break. As Mary uncoiled from mom's car, she excitedly waved and came running over to tell me how she was going *"to see heaven today."*

Struck by what I thought I heard, I asked, *"You are anxious to see what?"*

A huge smile broke across this 4th grader's face as she repeated, *"I can't wait. I get to see heaven today!"*

I was not sure if I should report this troubling statement to the school counselor or contact the parent to see what might have sparked such a comment. As we approached the door to the cafeteria where all the children gather to wait for the first bell, Mary shuffled quickly past me, arms waving. The last thing I heard was, *"Hi **Evan**, did you miss me?"*

She couldn't wait to **see Evan**.

Can misunderstandings begin this innocently? Absolutely.

The Behavior Cycle

We all have a brain, and the function of that brain is to get us what we need. We select behaviors for the sole purpose of satisfying our basic human needs. This is the cycle of behavior that all humans have in common.

Based on what we *need* (must have)…
we determine what we *want* (desire),
we then choose a *behavior* (an action)
we think will get it for us.

The *feedback* we receive from our behavior choices (and there will always be feedback)
will tell us if we got what we wanted.
The *experiences* that come out of our behaviors
shape our *perceptions*
and form our *expectations* for how we think we need to behave in order to get what we want... next time.

And that cycle will repeat itself every time you choose a new behavior to get something you want (need). You will repeat this cycle more that 50,000 times a day.

EACH decision is a new opportunity to begin anew.

Habits are still Choices

When you ask some people why they act the way they do, the answer may be, *"That's just the way I am."* Such an answer implies a pattern of thinking, or some kind of programming, rather than an understanding that our behaviors are our choices, not our destiny. How easy it is to slip into a pattern of thinking or a cycle of behavior that serves only to suppress independent thought.

Every time you come to the crossroads between HABIT and CHANGE, understand that *your habits* are still *your choices*.

Failure is simply success that quit too soon.

A Universal Truth

Countries and cultures have been waging wars for centuries to claim the power to tell others how to live their lives. In the 4th century, St. Augustine, a powerful influence for the spread of Christianity throughout the world, was asked this question: *"Teacher, how do we live a life that would please God?"*

St. Augustine's response was as fundamental for the 4th century as it is for all mankind today. In seven words, he defined the role of all humanity; he characterized the role of leadership. In one sentence he revealed this universal truth: *"First choose to LOVE... then do whatever you want."*

YOU hold the power to LOVE... or to refuse to love.
YOU hold the power to choose happiness... or to choose misery.
YOU hold the power to Respond... or to React.
YOU hold the power to Accept... or to Escalate.

Self inflicted Wounds.

When a new experience comes into opposition with a past experience, a number of mental assessments occur in the blink of an eye to lay the groundwork for **internal conflict**. When these Intrapersonal conflicts are permitted to remain unresolved, they are acted out in our Interpersonal relationships. It is the nature of humans to seek out and thrive on positive and healthy relationships. While your internal conflicts can readily escalate into interpersonal conflict, it cannot happen *without your consent.*

First understand that internal conflict is as perfectly natural as sunshine and water and need not always be viewed as something negative. For even the importance you place on how good you look and on what to wear to school or work every day, can place you "in conflict." But how many times a day do you ask yourself: *"Am I doing what I want to do... what I believe is right, or am I doing what others want me to do?"* How many nights have you struggled with that question; fighting sleep because those "voices" within wouldn't let you rest?

Perhaps you have never considered this relentless pull against your will, this internal conflict, as self-induced, and therefore, self correcting. Perhaps you have never considered how you have been *choosing* to remain in opposition to your own thoughts. Give yourself a break. There will never be a shortage of people willing to judge you. They don't need your help.

There is a time for believing in yourself... that time is NOW.

Bubble UP

The need for keeping your "Bubble Up" is adapted from my martial arts days. The Bubble Principle is a concept that allows you to picture yourself living inside this very large, very invisible, protective bubble. Within the security of the bubble is the knowledge that nothing can hurt you... physically or emotionally... *without your consent*.

On the way to earning a black belt in karate, students are taught how to eliminate distractions. I am quick to tell people that I earned my belts on my knees. For every time I made a mistake, I had to get on my knees... in the "meditation position"... to purge "my bubble" of the distractions. This was a common practice to teach students that the source of power, patience, and peace, comes from within. For inside, once free from the cluttered thoughts and distractions that were picked up from the world, we could once again fall under the protection of the "bubble." Some have called this prayer. Over time, it not only becomes easier to do, it becomes a source of great comfort. For only from within will any of us ever truly discover confidence, joy, self-reliance, strength, and peace.

Wrap yourself in the mind set that within the protection of *your* bubble, nothing can hurt you... emotionally... without your consent. When the distractions of life mount, hit those knees, and purge your bubble. The confusion and indecision will melt away into clearer, more focused thinking. Bubbling Up is a leadership prerequisite.

"Bubble-up" willingly and often as there are no limits to the number of mistakes you can make or the number of people in your life that seem intent on robbing you of your spirit.

The SCHOOL PRINCIPAL

A school principal wears many hats. As a school administrator, you can be seen as anyone from Father Confessor to Captain Bly. Depending upon the age of the student, the principal is seen as a super hero or as the Terminator. Because the teachers don't see him (or her) in their classrooms every day, the principal *obviously* has nothing to do all day. He is seen as a strong advocate for the school or an anchor to the budget of the instructional staff. The principal speaks on behalf of the staff, in support of his students, and in defense of his school.

To the students in high school, the principal is often seen as the enemy, merely because he/she is an adult. In grade school, the principal may average 20 unsolicited hugs a day. When a worried or upset parent brings his or her concerns into the school, the principal is often the first to catch the ire.

If a child is happy, the parent can see the principal as the one providing structure. If the child becomes unhappy, as might happen if junior received a low grade, when district policy collides with student behaviors, or when someone's daughter is cut at cheerleader tryouts, the principal is "the villain" and the focal point for all that is wrong with education.

The principal has no equal in authority in the school building. Consequently, the principal has no peers. The principal is alone…physically and emotionally. His/Her decisions will be questioned and second guessed—Just Like Yours!

How hard is it for you to choose wisely when you feel alone?

The QUEST

Rumors (gossip) exist in every school or work place. In that elusive, unending *quest for understanding* our minds will stretch to accept almost anything plausible.

We hear of an incident or decision that happened without our direct involvement, opinion or consent...and filter it against our own perceptions of "truth" to determine the value of the information received. When we then claim to seek understanding, our biases or personal agendas may uncover only those facts relevant to our own interests. In doing so, our understanding joins with what we *believe* happened or what we think *should have* happened, to become what *must have* happened.

For those who may legitimately be seeking knowledge, it is truly a sight to behold to see how mature, completely stable, intelligent human beings can get so mired in gossip. It is amazing how anyone who claims to be "seeking understanding" can take a nugget of news and assume that *plausible* equates with *reasonable.* How gullible some people are to willingly exchange that for a running start across the *Chasm-of-Conviction* to state with such certainty, "*Darn, how could they?*" For many, however, it is an easy jump, because they choose not to carry any facts with them on their trip.

People are altogether too willing to accept what they *hear*, rather than trust in what they *know*.

CAUTION:
DEAD END Ahead

I believe there is a direct correlation between speed and duration. The more rapidly it takes someone to leap across the *Chasm-of-Conviction,* from speculation to assumption, the longer she (or he) will stay there. The longer she stays there, the less interest she (he) will have in ever returning to the land of *Discussion and Reality.*

If a person makes the leap and does so without the benefit of facts, there is a great likelihood that she will be content to use the Chasm as a buffer to shield herself from the facts that now remain...conveniently...beyond her grasp.

The longer she remains on that side of the Chasm, she will remain in opposition to the receiving of facts. In fact (no pun intended), the longer she refuses to accept a helping hand to cross back over, the greater the likelihood that she will take root there, holding her preconceived notions and convictions indefinitely. And to meet her need for acceptance, she will do her best to drag others to that side of the Chasm to share in her misery. The longer she stays and the more allies she recruits, the longer the conflict will remain.

To establish a rapport; to open a line of communications with "difficult" people, do not speak...listen. The more you are willing to *listen*, the longer you will delay the "leap across the chasm."

The mind will create what it does not understand.

Whatever we mere mortals lack in understanding, we seem to make up for in imagination. The more intense an individuals "need-to-know" the more vividly the imagination can create whatever he/she *want*s to believe. As the mind further speculates in the absence of knowledge, the emotional distress will give way to very real physical aches and pains. Painful internalization of unacted upon thoughts will actually immobilize you.

What a leader chooses to imagine can be more destructive than what the leader actually does.

REACT or RESPOND?

If a doctor tells you that you are having a *reaction* to your medication, you know you're about to break out in hives. If the doctor tells you that you are *responding* to the medication, you know you're getting better.

In the same way, your decisions to either *react* (without thought) or *respond* (as one with a plan) will make all the difference in whether or not you are making decisions for yourself, or if you are granting permission for others to make your decisions.

**Leaders can either REACT to the behaviors of others,
or RESPOND to the needs that lie behind the behaviors.**

I HATE MY JOB

Let's say that you really do hate your job. Let's say that the difficulty you face at work, the reason you hate your job is... say... a co-worker; a staff member. A reasonable response to a difference of opinion might be to go directly to that person to resolve misunderstandings or misperceptions. Or you can follow through on the grievance process established by most companies and school systems to resolve conflict. Ultimately, you will choose to **respond** in only one of three ways *if* you want to resolve your conflict:

1. You can choose to accept— *even if you do not approve* of this person's behavior, personality, opinions, or whatever it is you find disagreeable.

2. You can choose to cooperate with this person to change that which you find to be disagreeable, i.e., cooperate, negotiate, assist, understand, etc.

3. Or you can choose to quit...choose to separate from this relationship, this team, this school, this district... this job.

Sorry, but that's it.
Anything else would be a reaction.

"Danger, Will Robinson!"

Remember the days of low budget television? I recall a particularly low budget, unimaginative series called, *Lost in Space*. The Robinson family was forever doomed to a fate of fending off Dr. Smith and one creature after another as they struggled, week after week, to bring their lost spacecraft back to earth. As with every other noted outer space drama, this show had a non-human, in this case, a robot, that played a supporting role as one of the mainstays of the story.

This robot had a dry wit but genuine charm. In one particular episode, I remember young Will Robinson was trying to hide from the monster of the week behind a wall decoration that had the appearance of a gigantic Halloween mask. Before eventually facing this demon (it was only an hour show), the robot (imaginatively named, "Robot") swiveled, and in that endearing monotone, admonished our hero with, *"You can't hide behind that mask forever, Will Robinson."*

To survive emotionally, you and I have built-in sensors, just like that robot. Just like Will Robinson, we recognize that we, too, hide behind masks but that we can't realistically hope to hide behind them forever. The purpose of our masks, of course, is to hide behind defensive walls, to shield our egos, to protect our feelings from a seemingly uncaring world. We also use masks to conceal our attempts to get what we want when others tell us we can't have it. Without the masks, we would have to be blunt and honest all the time. WHOA, who could take that?

You can, however, find peace when you are
consistently honest with others and yourself.

YOU hold the POWER

Because you live in a world with people in it, you already realize how your choices of behaviors can create internal and interpersonal conflicts that separate you from your friends, family, customers, and clients. You know the anxiety and the discomfort this places upon your spirit, a spirit that would much prefer to live in peace, than conflict.

When you make a simple oversight or mistake on a Monday, you often say, *"Oh, well, it's a Monday,"* or *"What do you expect for a Monday?"* You actually direct blame on a day of the week and allow a calendar to determine your mood.

Imagine walking down the hallway, and coming towards you is a person you don't like. Quickly you react by looking down at your watch, you pretend that something off to the side caught your eye, or anything to avoid "noticing" or having to speak to that person. You even have the fleeting thought of hitting the nearest exit and walking clear around the building rather than having to walk past *her* in this hallway. Amazing, isn't it? You just gave away your power to choose happiness...to *someone you don't even like!*

Now picture yourself driving down the street and someone cuts you off in traffic. You react by speeding up, getting right up there on his bumper, and if he stops in a hurry, you run into his car, become injured, and are cited for the accident! *YEAH...*that'll fix 'em! Now you've just given over your power to choose happiness to someone *you don't even know!*

You hold the power to resolve conflict.
Only You have the power to choose behaviors for You. Giving other people the power to make your decisions, makes as much sense as allowing a calendar to decide what kind of a day you're going to have.

Throw away the shovel

You may become angry as a result of what you have said or done...or may not have said or done. You can become angry when others refuse to do what you think they should say or do. Anger starts from within. The intensity of anger seems to grow when the level of expectations placed on others is not compatible with what others are willing to provide. Failed attempts to get others to give you what you want often sends you past irritation and frustration into anger.

As more and more withdrawals are made on your emotional bank, in failed attempts to find satisfaction, anger will manifest. Unresolved emotions will transcend into sarcasm and ridicule on the way to cynicism.

Cynicism is anger turned inward. Cynicism is a plea for help. It is the outward sign of a subconscious desire for somebody, anybody, to come to the top of the emotional well you may have thrown yourself into and to drop you a lifeline. Without that lifeline, it is a very short step from cynicism to depression.

Depression is not that difficult to identify. Watch for it. The three most obvious signs are S-L-S: Sadness, Listlessness, and Sleepy (the desire to sleep away the emotional exhaustion; to prevent the emotional bank from going bankrupt). Food and drink become the "medication" of choice.

Anger that leads to depression is *not* caused by others. It is instead an internal reaction to outside stimuli. You hold the power to respond, rather than react to the stimuli in your environment.

Never forget the first law for how-to-get-out-of-a-hole you dug yourself into: stop digging and throw away the shovel.

The Gift

Conan Doyle, the author of the Sherlock Holmes classics, claimed that his motivation for such an astute detective was inspired by the real life observation skills of Dr. Joseph Bell, his college professor. It was Dr. Bell (not Sherlock) who wrote, *"We are a people that see but we do not observe. Because we do not observe, we see one to be no different than another. Because we see one to be no different than another, we see others to be no different than ourselves."*

When it comes to understanding and accepting human behavior there is at least one constant:
the more we are different, the more we are exactly alike.

**The gift we offer each other
is NOT in UNDERSTANDING
that we're different,**

**the gift is in ACCEPTING
that we're different.**

Mixed Messages

A parent makes every attempt to teach a child honesty, integrity, and even tact. We say this is our intent, yet we model something else. We smoke in front of the child but warn them not to; we use colorful language and wash their mouth out for it; we tell them to 'play nice' while they listen to us berate our neighbor. And we realize we do this because we actually have an expression for it: *"Do as I say, not as I do."*

In front of Aunt Sadie, the parent says to the child who obviously did not like Aunt Sadie's gift, *"You should say thank you to Auntie for the gift."*

When Aunt Sadie leaves, the parent says to his spouse, *"That really was an ugly sweater from Aunt Sadie."* The parent turns to the child and says, *"You should be grateful for the gift."*

Later that night the parent says to the child, *"I know you didn't like it, but you can't tell people the truth."*

At bedtime, the parent leaves the child with, *"We won't tell Aunt Sadie; we'll take it back to the store tomorrow."*

Did the child understand the *words* of the parent? Probably.

Did the child understand the *intent* of the parent because the parent understood? Not sure.

Is it more likely that the parent just *assumed* the child would understand? More than likely.

So what did the parent actually TEACH the child????

Do you think the child got the message? What message would that be?

"Should" the child understand the message merely because the *parent* understands it?

Are YOU sending Mixed Messages?

We are not smarter than children...but we ARE more experienced.

We adults have become so comfortable with the masks that we wear. We wear them, of course, to shield our emotions from others. Through our experiences...our successes *and* our failures...we adults have become rather proficient at being polite when we would rather pout or feign the smile of acceptance in the face of rejection. These are defenses we learned as children.

As a result, as highly educated, multi-facetted, vastly experienced, mature parents and teachers, we adults still fail to understand why the chasm grows between ourselves and our children. We stubbornly, even defiantly refuse to step outside of *our* world of experiences and understanding to accept the obvious: Children do **not** know what we know. We actually get angry with children because they don't know what we know; because they aren't doing what we expect them to do, or to think, or to say.

If you want your instructions understood...
don't assume anyone knows what you know.

Don't assume understanding or hope for it...
TEACH it.

DISTRACT and DIVIDE

If you still choose to persist in *reacting* to your conflict, rather than choosing more appropriate *responses*, you are about to take your Internal conflict to another level. Venting your anger, frustration, and disappointments on others is a way to avoid having to deal with your problem. It is like saying: *"If I ignore what is troubling me, maybe it will go away."*

Reacting rather than responding is our inability, or stubborn unwillingness, to seek real solutions. We are employing avoidance behaviors when we continue only to hope for, rather than work for, closure to our conflicts.

Strategies to distract (avoid) and divide (separate) are evident in your telling and retelling of your "side of the story," your own particular perception of "what happened." Casting blame and accusations on others is a well established pattern to garner temporary relief and will, indeed, serve to bring you comfort and support. *But it will only do so for a while.*

Your conflict must be addressed to be resolved.
You can't rationalize your way to a resolution.

RELATE:
The root word of Relationship

The degree to which you are successful is dependent upon your ability to relate to others... to help others be successful. "What I am at any given point in my life, is in direct proportion determined by my connection with others; with those who love me or refuse to love me, with those I love or care about, or refuse to care about... or even acknowledge." —Harry Sullivan.

The early 20th Century psychologist and psychiatrist C. G. Jung first studied with Sigmund Freud. Jung dedicated his entire life to understanding the similarities and differences of others. These are his responses to what are referred to as the two universal questions.

1. What motivates ALL people to act the way they do? Their desire or inward need to be ACCEPTED; to be made to feel a part of their peer group. Consequently, people respond to the way others *want* them to, rather than what they would *prefer* to do. This is the basis for the conflict within —guilt, anger, resentment, etc.

2. What do ALL people have in common? That desire to be AFFIRMED. The need to be wanted, loved, and fulfilled.

Leaders are those who are willing to look past the negative and often irritable behavior of others, to recognize the NEED that others are seeking.

Acceptance is an Action Verb

Conflict is the uneasy feeling that you "forgot" something. It is that feeling that you may have embarrassed yourself at the party. It is wondering what to say to your teenager that won't upset him/her *this* time. It is the voice within that tells you how uncomfortable you are with the poor relationship that exists with your co-worker, spouse or child. Internal conflict is the knot in your stomach that tightens every time you think about what you "should have" said or "ought to do."

Many of us are being asked to meet higher quotas, raise test scores, do more with less, and do it faster and better then we did last month or last year. The increased stress serves only to highlight our internal conflict and heighten tension with co-workers (faculty and staff) and clients (students and parents). Our unresolved *internal* conflicts are at the root of our I*nterpersonal* conflicts; conflicts that sap our energy, divide relationships, separate teams, and rob us of our willingness to meet the increasing demands of work, home, and family.

**The acceptance of conflict can be as natural as conflict itself:
It requires effort...but leads to peace.**

Rumors are stronger than Reality

A lesson about the **power** of rumors.

There was a marvelous little web site entitled "Rumor Headquarters." The first paragraph of each article it published started with such disclaimers as, *"The following story is false; we made it up. This story is not true, it couldn't possibly be true, and we are stating for the record that it did not happen."* The article would then describe some plausible event that was tied to some current issue in the news. At the end of the article, you could read the surveys that had been conducted and the responses from readers.

As high as 40% of the respondents not only would swear it was the truth, many would add their own "evidence" in support of what the very first paragraph admitted was another blatant attempt from "Rumor Headquarters" to deliberately misrepresent facts.

TRUTH it would seem is in direct proportion to what we perceive... not what we know.

With a little help from my friends...

At one time or another, we all have experienced the relief that comes with confiding in another human being. We realize it as a gift of life.

We begin the shift from life-*draining* to life-*giving,* and say we feel a great weight lifted when we can *"bare our souls."* When we can think out loud, and place our ideas and fears in a safe and non-judgmental environment, we say it feels great *"to get it off my chest."* We know that our willingness to share and to open ourselves to others doesn't mean that we're weak or that we're "nuts." We are simply being permitted to test our thoughts against the patterns of thought that can be found in others. When we open up to others, we can find ourselves—in others. In this is the gift of life.

Where there is Trust, there is Peace.

Honor or Opportunity

One of the most basic of human needs, is the need to be Affirmed: to be understood, to be taken seriously, and *to be really LISTENED* to. When someone is depressed, rejected, angry, disappointed, or otherwise full of emotion, they *need* to be heard. They will seek someone that they believe will *really* "listen to me." What an honor that would be if they would choose YOU.

Perhaps you never saw this as a privilege. Imagine one of those times when YOU really needed someone *"to listen to me."* You didn't just grab the first person off the street, you didn't select just any colleague, acquaintance, family member or friend. You were about to share secrets; personal aspects about yourself that you certainly didn't want just anyone to know. Some might think you weak, lower their opinion of you, lose trust in you, or worse… tell others. You sought out someone YOU could trust… someone YOU respected… someone whose opinion mattered.

At one time or another, you will find yourself being asked to listen. Because we ALL have a human need to be heard… will you accept this as an honor or will you see this encounter only as an opportunity to be heard yourself? We want to share our own story, offer advice, to console, to condemn or otherwise make our own case; to tell someone about *my* day, show pictures of *my* grandchildren, tell someone about *my* life, *my* loves, *my* needs!

How do you see it? An Honor or Opportunity? Choose wisely.

A word about RUMORS

While rumors may contain some elements of "truth," rumors cannot substitute for, nor are they—**truth**. Rumors seem to be made up of perceptions of truth, inklings of facts, a sprinkle of excitement, and a trace of the cloak and dagger. Mix in a dash of the controversial, images of the confessional, equal amounts of surprise and indignation, and rumors are born.

Those starved for understanding and acceptance themselves, anxious to know "the truth," mark the hapless victim of their tale as guilty and often before he or she is aware that they were even "on trial." An individual's actual guilt or innocence takes a back seat to the seeds of doubt now planted in the community, gleefully shared by all those "in the know."

**Sadly, any explanation on the part of the victim
will now be seen only as defensive remarks
intended to cover up "the real truth..."**

The BUCK stops here.

There is one in every organization. He now stands in front of you. He is waiting for you to react. Like a dog patiently waiting for a pat on the head, the office gossip lingers after dropping his bone. Your very next word will determine if you will become a participant or a spectator in this latest round of idle chatter.

Do you want to perpetuate this or end this? Does this guy (gal) just want to be someone "in-the-know," or is he somehow being hurt in all this and is seeking a confidant? That is, is he coming to you because he wants your acceptance of him and his self-imposed role as the town crier, or is he seeking direction to resolve some conflict of his own? To know for sure, give him this One Sentence Response... and wait for your answer. With genuine sincerity, respond with:

"Really? So what did she say when you told her that?"

Often, a stunned and blank expression will follow your question. No, it probably wasn't the response he was looking for... but it may well be the response he needed. If he fumbles for an awkward answer, it may be because he had no intentions of going to the source of his concern or the subject of his rumor. Perhaps he just wanted to be the bearer of gossip to someone who was not as much "in-the-know" as he. If this is the case, you can pretty well count on the fact that he (she) will not be bringing future tales of gossip and woe to you as this clearly was not what you were "supposed to" say.

Do you want the Truth...or the REAL Truth?

You've got to love that oxymoron "...the real truth." The clue is in the implication that there is somehow more than one **truth**. When someone carries this phrase to you, look for the red flag warning you that this person has decided that whatever you might have believed to the contrary, she now has the *real* stuff.

There will **always** be differing versions of what *may have*... or may *not* have happened. Everyone will bring their own experiences, their own perceptions of how life "should be" into every situation. Because there will always be more than one side to a story, there will always be more than one way to see "the real truth."

When you are on the receiving end of a rumor (otherwise known as gossip), you are being asked to buy into something that may or not be based on fact. More than likely, it is based on something like this: *"I heard it from Mary, who heard it from Julie, who heard it at the mall, so it **must** be true."*

The REAL truth: The more a rumor is repeated the more weight it will carry and the more distance it will travel from "The Real Truth."

Out of the mouths of babes!

A little girl stood forlorn in her living room staring through the picture window out into the rain. Her father sat quietly in his chair reading his magazine, feeling sad that his young daughter could not go outside to play with her friends. *"I'll tell you what, honey,"* he said, *"in this magazine I'm reading there is a picture of the world. What if I cut this picture into several pieces and make a puzzle for you? Would you like that?"*

"Yes, Daddy," she said, and sat down on the floor by the side of the chair and began working on the puzzle her father had created for her. Meanwhile, father went back to his chair, content that the puzzle would keep her busy for quite some time. In just a few minutes, however, she stood up, smiled, and said, *"Daddy, I'm finished."*

Without looking, Dad smiled and said, *"Honey, you can't be finished yet; there are a lot of pieces to the world."*

"No, Daddy," she proclaimed, *"You don't understand. On the other side was a picture of children. I just put the children together, and the world took care of itself."*

Each one of us can intellectually accept that we can't change the world. To change the world, therefore, we must change the way we LOOK at the world.

Seek and you shall find.

We want to know who our children's friends are. We warn them not to run with *those kids*. If a child disobeys, we are quick to point out how the *other* children were a negative influence. We make excuses for them. We don't just protect our children; we shelter them. We want to keep them innocent; we want to keep them from harm…both physically *and* emotionally. We want to keep them from growing up…and leaving us. We want them to be happy.

What better way to guard our children from life's unpleasantness but to keep them from growing up for as long as possible. We tend to do *for* our children, rather than allowing our children to learn on their own. It is safer, and it is easier… to choose their friends, to justify their mistakes, to make excuses for inappropriate behaviors, to seek blame rather than ownership, to make exceptions to the rules, and to make decisions for children who are more than capable of choosing for themselves.

As parents and educators, we tell ourselves that the goal is to raise responsible adults. When it becomes more apparent that the goal is merely to "keep then happy," we are reduced to raising perpetual children.

Ownership for Actions

As a school principal, I once called a parent and asked her to join her son and me in my office. When the parent arrived, she stormed into my office. The first words out of her mouth were, *"It wasn't my child. He couldn't possibly have done this!"* After only a momentary pause, her face revealed her conflict before next breaking the silence with, *"Just what is he being accused of anyway?"*

We want our children to be happy...to love us...but at what price? This mom was so willing to save Johnny from his poor choices...to deflect blame from her child...that she couldn't even wait to find out why he was there before trying to rescue him.

We want our children to be responsible citizens, to be caring, to love their siblings, and to obey their parents. And we would probably want them to admit when they were wrong and to accept the consequences (rewards and punishment) for their actions. But what message do we send them? How can we *teach* them wrong from right if we refuse to set and follow boundaries; if we prevent them from understanding that there are consequences for unsafe or inappropriate actions? Would that not also apply to the adults we supervise?

The longer you refuse to allow others to accept ownership for their actions, the clear, but unspoken message is:
"You do not have to be accountable for your behavior."

Setting Boundaries

When *asking* children to obey is not enough, parents routinely attempt to control (rather than provide consistent boundaries). We often employ threats and intimidation, *"I'm not going to tell you again! I'm going to (send you to your room, not give you ice cream, keep you at that table until you eat your dinner, etc. ...")* When we fail to follow up, we reinforce the child's confusion: particularly when we extol them with, *"I really mean it this time!"*

When you do not teach boundaries, clear and consistent consequences for behaviors, people are *still* learning. They are not learning the lessons you wanted...but rest assured, they are still learning. They are learning that you have no boundaries, or the boundaries you have are set in jello, not concrete, and that what you say is not what you mean. In the absence of consistent boundaries and consequences, those whom you serve, learn fear, confusion and uncertainty.

People do not just **want** structure in their lives; they will *insist* upon it. In the absence of clear boundaries, people *will* act out until they get them...guaranteed!

When it comes to setting boundaries,
there is absolutely NO difference
between being a parent, and being a LEADER.
The results will be the same.

It's All about ME

Every organization has an employee who disagrees with the direction leadership has taken. Often, he (she) will withhold cooperation as a way of making that statement. He may criticize, lay blame and withhold to reclaim the acceptance and belonging he believes he's lost. As a result, he will come across as arrogant, self-centered, cynical and "All about ME." In his mind, however, he is desperate: an injustice has been done and it has become his mission to right the wrong.

Unfortunately, the approach he has taken to being heard will serve only to further alienate the very people from whom he seeks acceptance. He does not realize that everyone else's "All about ME" attitude naturally resist being forced to do something… even if it's the right thing to do.

The leaders among us, therefore, must be willing to look past their own defensiveness to stop taking such behaviors personally. Leaders must look beyond the moment to see the larger picture. If it will help, ask yourself, *do you want this person working for you or against you?* This employee wants only to be accepted: taken seriously, understood, and really listened to. (*Just like you!*) **Want to pull him in? Follow these two steps… and in this order:**

1. *Listen* **to him:** He *needs* to be heard… so *listen* to him. Leave your defensiveness at the doorstep and just *listen*. Invite him to lunch, take him to tea, sit with him in the break room, take a walk, but *hear* him out! He has been thinking about this for a long time… so prepare to dedicate some time.

2. *Find* **a** *part* **for him in the** *project*: He needs to be accepted, included, and reunited with his peers. He is beyond asking… but he is not beyond *accepting* your invitation to participate in something for which he may have a particular talent.

He needs to renter peer relationships: he needs you to open the door.

Rumors

We come back to Rumors. They swirl around us like the wind. We love them...we hate them. We *love* to take a part, to hear it all, to be included in the group, to be the first one on the block to "know" the guff on our neighbors.

We *hate* it when we are the topic of that rumor.

We know rumors hurt. That pain is real. But the human Need to be accepted can overpower common sense. The knot it leaves in our stomach, when we are alone, reminds us.

Where do you stand on the subject? Organizations can rise or fall on idle gossip. Rumors will take root in the absence of clear, concise and open communications.

For the Leader, the choice. . . as it has always been. . . is YOURS.

People are watching. . . and listening.

Change is a Choice

People **decide** to adopt new behaviors. That is, we "change" behaviors for one of two reasons: we *want to* or we believe our options are limited and we *have to*.

In fact, both are choices. Even when our backs are to the wall and our emotional or even our physical survival depends on it, we may still try to disguise our decision and save face by saying we were *forced* into it.

If you are on the threshold of a major change in your life, first decide to take ownership for the reason for the change. Then open your mind to change. You can start by leaving your judgments, preconceived notions, and heavy emotional baggage at the doorway to your mind. Wipe thoroughly, making certain that you leave BIAS and FEAR on the mat beneath your feet. With nothing to lose, and everything to gain, crack open the door to your mind. Take the Risk. Shed any false pride that still clings to you. Take a deep breath... and prepare to step into faith.

NO ONE can take this next STEP but YOU.

Seeing is Believing

A kindergarten teacher saw one of her students furiously at work drawing a picture at her desk. When the teacher stepped over to where she was working, she asked the little girl what she was painting. Without hesitation, the little one proclaimed, *"I'm painting the face of God."*

Amused, the teacher said, *"That's wonderful, dear, but no one has really ever seen the face of God to know what He looks like."*

As if shocked by the teacher's remarks, the child glanced down at her drawing...then looked back up at the teacher. Once again she looked at her drawing, then back up at the teacher. Finally, with quiet confidence, the little girl insisted, *"They will when I'm finished!"*

Confidence is not boastful, proud or arrogant. Confidence is not being right...to prove others wrong. Confidence is having the courage to believe in yourself...admitting when you're wrong...and having the courage to try again (and again, and again, and...).

The Golden Rule

Mark Twain once said, *"Always tell the truth. It will shock some people and amaze the rest."*

With all due respect to Mr. Twain, **never** assume someone's "facts" as "truth." At least some aspect of everyone's story is probably just that…a story. A story is not a lie, or a fabrication, or even a "fib." It can be someone's legitimate perspective on what happened.

No matter how many "sides" there are in a conflict, all parties can only offer their own version of what they believe…or what they *want* to believe. Each of us can only offer his or her own understanding or perception of what happened based on first-hand knowledge, past experiences with such events, and even how each person defines the vocabulary used to describe the event. Somewhere in the blending of all perspectives, of the telling and retelling of the story, is "truth."

The Leader must make a determination. If an employee is at fault, admit it. Deal with it appropriately and as quickly as possible. When you build a reputation for being honest, your **word** will stand for something. Someday you will have to tell your critics what they don't want to hear. They won't like it, but they will be compelled to accept it…because you have been consistent; because you will have earned the *right* to be trusted.

The Golden Rules for Leaders
Never say anything that you wouldn't want published in the newspaper and make every decision as if you were explaining it from the witness stand.

Always and Never

South Bend, Indiana is probably best known as the home of Notre Dame University. Many of us grew up on Notre Dame football. Years ago my father, in trying to offer a lesson to me on the virtues of honesty, relayed this story about a young football player from Notre Dame by the name of Frank Symanski. Over the years I have shared this story many times.

Frank, a normally shy young man, was called upon to be a witness in a civil suit in the South Bend courtroom. As Frank took the stand, the judge could see the young man's apprehension and attempted to put him at ease:

"I hear you are on the Notre Dame football team, Mr. Symanski."

"Yes, sir, Your Honor, I am."

"What position do you play?" asked the judge.

"I play Center, Your Honor."

"Are you any good in that position, Mr. Symanski?"

Pausing for a moment, obviously uncomfortable, Frank confidently replied, *"Sir, I'm the best Center that ever played for Notre Dame."*

Frank's coach was in the courtroom and was visibly taken aback by what might have seemed to be a boastful response from his normally reserved athlete. When the session was over, the coach asked him why he had made such a statement.

A bit surprised by the question, the embarrassed young man gave an honest reply. *"I hated to do it, Coach, but I was sworn to tell the truth, the whole truth, and nothing but the truth."*

Always, even if your mother told you there is no such thing as always, always be honest with people and always tell the truth. When later asked to recall the event, it will be the easiest thing to remember.

Saving Face

Watch your back with people who seek to restore their fragile self-image. When they don't get their way, they may try to lift themselves up at the expense of someone else's credibility. When saving face becomes more important than the truth, do not expect such people to be open about it. As any coward would, they will try to garner empathy and support in their desperate attempt to cover their lies. You will know instantly that there is going to be more to the story than you are going to hear when they begin with something like, *"I'm telling you this in complete confidence."*

When the tale you are about to hear begins in such a way, Mr. Woe-is-me is now free to rewrite the event from what *actually* happened to whatever will allow him to feel better about himself.

And the greatest sadness is, the one you are allowing to be discredited may never know why *you* turned on him (her), too. He will never know why you won't speak to him anymore. For the instant you agreed to go under this secret blanket of darkness, you lost all hope that the TRUTH could ever be revealed.

Be on guard against people who are too willing to talk about others to you. You can bet the barn that this same person can't wait to talk to others about YOU.

So many BEHAVIORS: only five basic NEEDS.

When asked to do something for another, there is a part of us that says, *"What's in it for me: More pay, affirmation, a future favor?"* We choose behaviors to get us what we want. We tend to see other people's behaviors as obstacles to *"getting what I want!"*

We want to be first in line, we want to catch all the traffic lights green, we expect our lottery ticket to be **the** lottery ticket, we want what we want when we want it, we get angry when others tell us no, we actually expect everyone to agree with us… and we see **nothing** wrong with this. Consequently, a great source of our conflict stems from our inability **not** to see anything wrong with this.

The number of human behaviors is endless… but the number of basic human Needs can be counted on one hand. All behaviors are motivated by each person's conscious or subconscious desire to meet one or more of these five basic Needs:

Survival
Love and Acceptance
Affirmation and Fulfillment
Fun
Freedom

BEHAVIORS: (con't)

There is a vast difference between what you Need and what you Want. You choose behaviors you believe will get you what you want in an attempt to meet one or more of those Needs. And you will do this several thousand times a day.

It can be a great comfort for the leader to know that *I do not have to take someone else's behaviors personally.* Behaviors are simply each person's best attempt to meet one or more of their basic human Needs. *Others have simply chosen ME to help them meet their Needs.*

Learn to look *past* their behavior to understand what Need they are trying to meet. You can't always give them everything they want, but you can almost always give them some of what they Need.

Work to meet the Needs of others, and you will find others tripping over themselves to meet YOUR Needs and the most amazing part is, they will do it willingly, and they won't even know why they're doing it... Guaranteed!*

* Book 1—*"What did you do THAT for?"*

"... like holding wood under water."

Carl Jung said that trying to hold back the knowledge that is within you, that is, "trying to deny the truth," would be no different than trying to indefinitely "hold wood under water." You can hold it down for awhile, but the unconscious mind is unrelenting in its attempt to bring the truth to the surface.

One might be able to consciously suppress *some* thoughts or emotions, but the more one tries to hold them down, the harder it is to consciously keep covered whatever it is your unconscious mind is trying to reveal. The truth will always surface; if not consciously, your body language will betray the mind.*

Remember your first date? You told yourself (and your date) that you weren't nervous. Yet, you tripped over your tongue, spilled drinks, didn't know what to do with your hands, and your bumbling attempts to say good-night on the doorstep all spoke loudly to the contrary. Just as you can't forever hold wood under water, you can't forever suppress the **truth** that lies just beneath the surface. If you were nervous on that first date, as hard as you might have tried to suppress it, your body language could not lie—for it will *always* reveal *the knowledge within*.

Leaders are always seeking positive relationships and strong work teams. Leaders would do well to understand the messages both sent and received through body language and other non-verbal communications cues.

*(See seminars on this topic in the back of this book.)

The Monk and the Feathers

In a fourteenth century monastery, the Master had been attempting to teach his young student how all of life can be impacted by a single word or a single deed. *"THINK,"* He urged, *"before speaking."* The student could not imagine how the actions of one person, or one solitary life, could make such a difference. The Master continued, *"Once a word or action has been set into motion, it cannot be recaptured. Its impact will go on forever."* Still the student could not grasp his meaning.

The patient Master then told his student to take the pillow off his bed, walk it to the tower, and empty the contents from the top window of the tower. Obliging, though confused, the student did as he was asked. At the top of the tower, he took his down-filled pillow, opened the end, and shook its contents into the wind. He then walked back down the stairs to again face his Master.

"As you would cast your words into the wind, have you now cast the feathers into the wind?" asked the Master.

"Yes," replied the student, *"the wind now carries the feathers."*

"Now go," sighed the Master, *"return every feather to the pillow."*

Once your words and action are set into motion,
even the most sincere and gracious *"I'm sorry,"*
won't bring them back.

"YOU DON'T UNDERSTAND ME!"

A sixth grade girl entered an internet chat room and began conversing with *"a friend."* Sure, her teachers and parents told her not to, but it was fun and *"what could it hurt?"*

Mother became suspicious only after she noticed a change in her daughter's attitude and even in her vocabulary. Mother, of course, remembers distinctly telling her daughter that she *"should not"* get in those chat rooms, so Mom couldn't understand why her daughter would do that. Yet, Mom did realize that her daughter was spending too much time in *"those d—chat rooms"* but didn't want to say anything because *"I knew it would cause an argument."* Mom said she didn't want to risk *"making her angry."*

Mom was now frantic. She told the officer that she couldn't understand how *"things got so out of hand."*

Mother said she *"knew better"* but only wanted her daughter *"to be happy."* She had, after all, *"wanted to be her daughter's friend."* The mother was seeking love and acceptance from the daughter: the daughter was seeking her need for acceptance from this guy she met on line. Mother blamed herself. She told the officer that by not insisting on clear boundaries, she now understood that her daughter was ultimately betrayed by "her friend." Mother learned too late that her daughter had enough friends, she needed to be the parent.

"YOU DON'T (con't)

The fears being projected by Mom came out of her understanding of the world…out of *her* world of experiences. Mom drew her imagery from a lifetime of movies, books, warnings, words, pictures and more. She drew her fears from her associated experiences. Her experiences, the foundation for legitimate concern, were not adequately taught to the daughter.

The officer explained what was happening. As he did, mom's panic brought back her understanding of such words as *"child porn, manipulation, and rape."* She was beginning to realize that her 12-year-old daughter could not possibly have understood the dangers. How could a pre-teen be expected to have the extensive understanding, experiences, even the vocabulary comprehension of an adult?

Without such experiences or understanding, the daughter did not "see" the danger. The child could not relate to the potential for disaster. Mom could now understand just how right her daughter was each time she cried, *"You don't understand me!"*

The root of Relationship is to Relate.
As long as we refuse to step outside of our own world of understanding, our own pictures of how we think the world "should be," we cannot hope to Relate to co-workers, customers, clients or even to our own family members.

The Magic Blender

Every experience *you* have ever had—the car rides, the sandbox, the walks along the ocean, the toys you played with, the God you prayed to, every book, magazine article or passage you've ever read, the friends you had, the people who loved you…or *refused* to love you…and even the last couple of minutes you've dedicated to reading this, ALL go into the formation of you.

It is as if there was an invisible magic blender on the top of your head. This blender serves to mix up every new experience you receive, blending and mixing with all those other experiences, so that what comes out of you, with each new experience, makes you even *more* unique than you were just a few moments before. Every *second* is a new opportunity to make new choices! Your choices come out of **your** world of understanding—and are right for *you*.

Do you remember that expression, *"The more we're different, the more we're exactly alike?"* While most of us would agree that we are different from each other, what we are *really* saying under our breath is not, I am different from you, but that "**You** are different from **me**."

It is as if each of us is saying, "**I am the standard**" by which all humans are made, and anyone different from me…is…well, obviously…wrong! We then dedicate a lifetime in the attempt to get others to see the world as we *want* it to be…as **we** think it *should* be.

Different, however, does not mean other people are wrong. It does mean they are going to be different than you…and that's O.K.!

You want it... TEACH it.

Remember when your mom said, *"Don't touch the stove, it's hot!"* Sure enough, you had to test it for yourself. Was it because you couldn't trust your own mother? Or was it because you had no experience to compare? The last time mom said "hot," maybe she was referring to a "hot" sunny day. Your mind didn't, at that time, differentiate between "hot" and (a word you'd soon be learning...), scalding.

Your previous experiences said "hot" is not so bad, so what's the big deal? But *after* you touched the "hot" stove, the *feedback* you received (...and there will always be *feedback*), planted *new* pictures into your memory bank; pictures with labels like Pain, Fear, Trust Mother, and *Bad* Stove.

When Dad said "*Do not* ride your bike in the street." Did he **teach** his child what he wanted, or like mom, did he just **tell** his child what was hoped for? What else is he to do with a child who has no comparable experiences?

Dad, of course, may have once fallen off his bike, been scared by traffic, seen a movie about someone on a bike being hit by a car, or in any one of a few dozen ways *experienced*, and now *knows*, that this is dangerous. Dad learned by experience.

In Junior's absence of such experiences, will just *telling* him to keep his bike out of the street get Dad's message across? How many times have *you* said (or have your parents said to *you*), *"Don't make me tell you again!"* Or *"If I have to say this one more time..."*

The lesson here is obvious:
Because you SAID it...it does not mean they "get it."

Words are the Labels

When words come to us, our mind requires no preparation to receive them. Words are nothing more than labels for the pictures in our mind. Once offered, without conscious thought, the mind races to match labels to experiences in order to give context to the message.

Instantly, the mind creates perceptions, finds amusement, makes judgments, asks questions, or otherwise seeks further understanding of what was heard, or read. And when we are not sure what is intended, we *imagine* we know what was intended, implied, offered, or inferred.

**We forget that communication (understanding)
is NEVER in the *intent* of the speaker,
but ALWAYS in the message received by the listener.**

Controlling Behaviors

In Asia, in order to capture a monkey, you build a small cage and stake it to the ground. You then put a banana in the cage and wait. Soon, a monkey will come by, squeeze his hand between the bars, and grab the banana. To avoid capture and ultimately being boiled for dinner, the monkey has only to release his grip, pull his hand back, and run away. His *refusal* to release control of the fruit is what will lead to his capture... *and ultimately,* to his death.

Behaviors to control begin when someone tells you "No" but you refuse to take "No" for an answer. Behaviors used to control, that is, to manipulate the behaviors of others, are referred to as Controlling Behaviors. We all do it to some degree and can do so without risking conflict with self or others. (How do you think Tom Sawyer got those other kids to whitewash that fence for him?)

Most Leaders, for example, know that in order to maintain authority, they must at times *release* control (of decisions, programs, and committees), in order to maintain authority.

If you intend to hold onto the banana, for fear that someone might get it if you let go, or if you believe that you are the only one within your organization capable or trustworthy enough to grasp the prize, then you will be managing (not to be confused with Leading) by control. If you want what you cannot have or fear you will lose what you have, you will figure ways to *control* people to give you what they didn't want you to have. It's OK, and natural...up to a point.

When you become fixated on what you want and can't have, psychologists refer to this as LOSS of INSIGHT; like a monkey that would rather die than release control of what is within his grasp.

Just another day?

It was nearly twenty years ago, but I still remember an article I read that was written by the late syndicated columnist, Sydney Harris. He was relating an incident he and his friend had at a local newspaper stand and it went something like this:

He said he and his friend walked up to the paper stand where they patiently waited for service. Finally, as they were approached by the attendant, they were addressed in almost an accusatory tone, *"What do ya' want?"*

The man with Sydney Harris responded, *"I would like to have a copy of the London Times, please."*

"Just a minute!" came the abrupt response. The man returned a minute later, slapped the paper on the counter and snapped, *"That's six bits."* The friend offered the money to the attendant and received a cold, *"Hold on"* as he turned to make change. After a few moments the attendant returned, sliding the change across the counter without a word.

"Thank you," the friend directed to the man who had already turned around and moved away. He recovered his change from the counter and turned to leave. As Sydney Harris and his friend moved away from the stand, Sydney stopped his friend and questioned, *"Wait a minute, I've got to know something. Do you come here everyday for a newspaper?"*

"Yes," replied his surprised friend. *"Everyday. Why?"*

"I have got to know something; does that man treat you like that everyday?"

"Yes," his friend answered, *"I'm afraid he does."*

"Now I really need to know, how can you take that? He was just rude and hateful, and you even said, 'Thank you' for that!? Doesn't the way he treats you make you angry?"

The friend was surprised, and stared at Sydney as if the answer was obvious. His response was classic, and the perfect validation of the fact that all behaviors are choices, when he said,. *"I don't want him to decide what kind of day I'm going to have."*

Who decides what kind of a day you're going to have?

And a little child shall lead them...

If you tell a child **NO**, you can't have this thing you want.... you have just taught the child a **boundary**. Expect, then, the boundary to be pushed, *"Please, I really want this thing you won't let me have!"*

If you next say (or eventually say), *"Oh, O.K., I give up, you can now have this thing you want that I said you could not have,"* what did you really teach the child?

You have taught the child that "No" means "Yes." The child has further taught **you** that to get his/her boundaries moved, all he/she has to do is wear you down! And because you have moved them, the child knows you will move them again. Until structure (boundaries) are taught and you, too, are willing to follow them, don't expect behaviors to change.

Learn from your children. Your employees have.
For what we know as adults...
we have learned as children.

You want to change the World?

First and foremost comes the knowledge that **all** change begins from within. No, you can't change the world…but you *can* change the way you *look* at the world. You want to change the world? Change your mind.

If you really want to change the world, it can be as easy…and as difficult…as changing the way you've been viewing your world. You can stop seeing the world the way you want it to be, and begin accepting it the way it is.

It can be as easy as being open to change… and allowing yourself to *be c*hanged. Try not to anticipate, and certainly not to expect changes in others. A change in others will occur, but that won't happen… it cannot happen… until you first realize a change in the most important person in your life…you.

You will recognize the seeds of change have been planted
the first time you are willing to ACCEPT...
even when you don't agree.

You will *always* have CHOICES

Control begins when someone tells you NO!
Conflict begins when you won't take NO for an answer.

"*NO! You can't have whatever it is you wanted. It is **mine**, and I don't want you to have whatever it is **you** think you want and **should** have. It is **not** yours to take, I'm **not** giving it to you, the answer is **no**, and that's final!*"

"What's that you say? But I always get what I **want**! Perhaps you didn't hear me. I **want** this thing that you won't let me have!"

From the crib, we have been hearing NO... but at any age, we still can't accept it. This scene is played out hundreds of times every day, generation after generation, yet the **options** never change. Each and every time you hear "NO" you will then choose: "Will I *respond* or will I *react?*" Each time your response is NO (and each time you are confronted with a NO, from your employees, customers, spouse or teenager), you *will select* from one of the following **two** options:

1. You will *accept* that you can't have what you want...*this time.* This whatever it was that you wanted that someone else possessed and doesn't want you to have. You are now open "to **want**" something else.

OR

2. You will *escalate* by choosing *Controlling* Behavior to get what you want even though you've already been told "*NO, you CAN'T have this thing you want.*"

THAT'S IT.... these are your ONLY two choices.

The Escalation of Control

People will tell you "No." Count on it...make plans for it...it is one of life's guarantees. When that time comes, you will either Accept...or Escalate to control the other into giving you this thing you want that they won't let you have. If you choose no for an answer...to escalate control to ultimately possess this thing you cannot have...it may look something like this:

Level 1: When someone tells you "No"—You can respond by...
Accepting "No" for an answer, even if you don't agree,
or change behaviors to seek something else. If you choose to Escalate, you will escalate and **react by**:
Choosing a behavior intended to *control* to get what you want, i.e., crying, pouting, guilting, stomping your feet, slamming doors, etc.

Level 2: If someone still says "No" – You can respond by...
Accepting "No" for an answer, even if you don't agree,
or change behaviors to seek something else, If you choose to Escalate, you will escalate and **react by**...
Increasing the level of *control:*
This raises the stakes by increasing the *level of pressure (Control)* exerted to acquire whatever it is you want.
It also increases the pressure on the relationship between you and the person who
won't let you have this thing you want.

Level 3: If someone still says "No" – You can respond by...
Accepting "No" for an answer (finally), even if you don't agree,
or change behaviors to seek something else, If you choose to Escalate, you will escalate and **react by**...

Escalation (con't)

Increasing the level of *control:*
This raises the stakes to subtle manipulation, non-verbal suggestions, and veiled implications.

Level 4: If someone still says "No" – You can respond by...
Accepting "No" for an answer, even if you don't agree,
or change behaviors to seek something else. If reasoning has failed to tell you that you can't **control** this human being, you will **react by**...further increasing the level of *control:*
This raises the stakes by releasing internal conflict into open hostility: relationships jeopardized, name calling, intimidation, prolonged displays of anger, threats and verbal attacks are evident.

Level 5: If someone still says "No" – You can respond by...
Accepting "No" for an answer, even if you don't agree,
or change behaviors to seek something else. If you choose to Escalate, you will escalate and **react by**...
further increasing the level of control:
As PRIDE forbids you from backing down, and REASON fails to tell you that PRIDE is also what is inhibiting him/her from giving into YOUR pressure, you will have reached the final level: .
Character assassination, alienation, sides formed with co-workers, family and community, walls are built, and a visible shift occurs from Conflict to *Violence.*

The lesson here: You can't control anyone, for any length of time, but you can ALWAYS be in control of YOU!

Fear of Rejection

If you have failed at something in the past, it is easy to fall back on that experience and assume that failure would follow you again into your future. Many fear that if they were to make another attempt, they would only fail…again. In fact, the choice of *"I'll NOT try again"* can be less frightening, even comforting, than having to endure the feelings that come from failure…one more time. Some would call this a "Self-fulfilling Prophecy."

Fear of rejection and loss of acceptance can polarize us. We adopt the adage, *"Better the devil you know than the one you don't know,"* rather than risk again. That is why some of us readily accept dead-end jobs or repressive relationships. If we have been hurt through past experiences, we might say to ourselves:

"Why take a chance on another attempt at seeking happiness when the misery I KNOW can be preferable to the risk I'd be taking?"

All Behaviors are Learned

Children, without the conscious understanding of the many nuances of voice inflection and body language, are only "works in progress." As a result, children are still beginners in their attempts to mask their intent and guard their emotions. This is why children are so much easier to read than we more sophisticated adults.

As children mature through puberty and adolescence, they model what they have learned through observation, discovery and practice. As children grow and mature, they become more adept at incorporating inflection and body language to meet their needs (and wants).

Children not only learn from us…they study us. They master the lessons. Pouting, crying, hugs, and smiles are all learned behaviors. They are quick learners. After all, without our help, how would our children ever learn to be sarcastic, judgmental, bigoted, and just plain mean to each other?

All behaviors are choices.
All behaviors are learned.
All behaviors can change.

The School

Consider the vast sea of insecure, hyper, excited, nervous, prepubescent adolescents that transform silent school buildings at 7 a.m. every morning, into loud, overcrowded classrooms, corridors, and gymnasiums by 7:30. They leave en masse at the end of the school day, many returning to empty homes and to unlimited Internet access. Most are subject to sexually explicit television programming that began long before they got home, will run through "prime time," and continue long after they were supposed to have drifted off to sleep.

Every child's overpowering human Need is for peer acceptance. They pull out those cell phones before their butts hit the bus seats and can't wait to reconnect later with their classmates on the telephone or on-line. The next morning, many without the benefit of breakfast, will re-board the same bus and will carry back to their classmates, everything that was said, implied, offered, or threatened the night before. They will meet to act out their fears, insecurities and excitement in the only place they will come together all week — in school. The teachers have prepared plans for the day...so have the kids.

Enter into our schools: CONFLICT

Watts in a Word?

You understand others… and others are left to understand you… in three ways: Through Words, Inflection and Body Language. Depending on what study you read, people most effectively are communicating their message 8 -11% of the time through their words; 13 – 37% of the time through voice inflection; and 50 – 80 % of the time through Body Language. We know that Words are the most ineffective way to communicate… yet this is where we most often place our ability to understand one another.

As a fisherman, I know that if I have a lure in my tackle box that will catch fish only 8-11% of the time, I would have to use it with something else in order to catch more fish. In the same way, Leaders must expand their tool boxes to include a deeper understanding of all the tools they will need to become more effective communicators.

Your body language speaks louder than your words.*

* See Seminars in the back of this book.

OOPS...

After 17 years, I returned to the school district where I began my teaching career. I returned as a school principal in an elementary school. During my first couple of weeks, it was not uncommon for most of the more than 400 children to pass me in the hall or come up to me on the playground and say, *"You taught my mommy or you taught my daddy."* (I was ok with that until they would say, *"You taught my grandma or my grandpa."*).

One day, one of my former students, Lois Black, came in to introduce me to her daughter, one of my 5th grade students. Later than day I saw another little girl in my school that looked a lot like Lois. Thinking Lois must have another daughter, I suddenly blurted out, *"Hey, I think I know your mommy. Are you a Black?"*

With only a moment's hesitation, she cocked her head and announced, *"No, I've always been white."*

Words do not convey understanding, yet understanding is assumed from our words. Through these obvious contradictions, the seeds of human conflict are planted. Words are not accurate measures of intent, yet intent is often assumed from our words.

Many of us readily accept whatever we *hear*, make instant judgments, provoke conflicts, even end relationships based solely on the words that come to us. As long as we put more faith in words, than in people, we will continue to empower conflict and allow three other words to rule our relationships: misperceptions, misunderstandings, and misinterpretation.

Words can only convey meaning, not intent.

"Don't hate the player, hate the game."

We call it "A Game."

To every guy or gal that has ever said, *"I'm not playing their game,"* understand that we are ALL participants in the game, whether we want to be players or not. It is not really *"their game"* that you object to, it is whatever *"strategy"* they are employing in their "game" to get what they want that bothers you. Leaders would benefit from reviewing some of "the games" and strategies people play:

Distract and Divide
The Rule of Opposites
One Sentence Responses
The Direct Approach

React or Respond
The Rumor Mill
The Bubble Principle

You can't control the game... but you *can* always be in control of YOU.*

* Book 2— *"So THAT'S why you're like that?"*

The Bucket Principle

It's not very flattering, of course, but visualize each person you meet as being a walking bucket full of... human Needs. That is, think of each person you meet as having the *same* human Needs for Love and Acceptance; Affirmation and Fulfillment: Fun; and Freedom, that YOU have. The pressures of work, the obligations of family, the weight of your responsibilities, the daily frustrations and anxieties of life in general that you carry... *every one else* feels too!

Now, walking your way is someone who wants to be heard... to ask YOU... *"will you listen to me?"*

A leader knows that if you want to be heard, you must first be willing to LISTEN. *Truly* LISTEN. Listening is not waiting for a pause to insert your own agenda, or thinking up clever responses while you wait for him/her to finish. Listening (not to be confused with hearing) is a decision. It is being willing to put aside your agenda, and dedicate some time to focusing on the speaker. Finding someone who will truly listen is rare. For many, this is the Gift of Life.

If you want to be heard, you MUST understand the Bucket Principle.

This principle accepts that the person who is coming to you to "be heard" is carrying a bucket full of emotions into this conversation. Understand that a full bucket means just that: it is already FULL. Your agenda, your advice, your counsel, even your words will NOT be accepted until you have allowed her to pour out some from her bucket first. You want to be heard? Then you must listen first. When it is your turn, her body language will reveal her relief... her satisfaction that finally... someone is truly *listening to me*.

If you don't permit her to pour out some of her concerns first, there will be no room in that vessel for anything you may want to add.

Always follow your Heart

My two favorite teachers are Dr. Linda Geronilla, and Sister Nancy Forkort. They never told their students *what* to think; they taught us *how* to think. Both taught incredible life lessons.

Sister Nancy helped me to understand the *"voices within."* She helped me to accept that the "voices" could be a comfort rather than a source of anxiety.

"Consider looking at it this way," she began. *"One voice is simply trying to lead you to good, while the other is trying to lead you astray. When in doubt, instead of struggling with them...separate them.*

The voice that tells you that you "should or ought" to do something, may well be telling you what you believe other people think you "should or ought" to do...or what you think others will say you "should" do. This voice is the 'JUDGE.' The only voice left is that of your heart.

"Always follow your heart."

Personal Responsibility

"You have the right to resolve the conflicts in your life. You have the right to meet your own needs. You have this right as long as you do not interfere with the rights of others to meet their needs."— Dr. Linda Geronilla

When you are finally ready to end an interpersonal conflict, particularly one that has dragged on for entirely too long, you are saying that you are finally ready to face your demon. It means you are ready to put an end to the emotional drain and the physical pain that this open wound has been causing you. The longer this has dragged on, the more baggage you must dump at the foot of the one you believe has hurt you. You have been storing up for this for a very long time and you have a right to say your piece.

The goal is to get over it; to get past it. Understand, however, that getting even is not getting past it; it will resolve nothing. Dumping is good...to a counselor, or to your mentor...but not onto the source of your pain.

If you are ready for the direct and honest approach, leave the baggage at the altar and *find your peace, rather than saying it.* Empty yourself of all that intends to sting. Share, explain, listen (allow the other to vent...because they have been carrying this around for a long time, too), and close the book on this. Once you get it out of you...even if the other does not want to accept your peace, this will be over for YOU...I promise!

**You have the right to resolve your conflicts with others.
With every choice, however, you have responsibilities.
This responsibility places you above illegal, immoral or
unethical behaviors to get what you want.**

Taking CHARGE

Into every leader's life comes the time to rethink his or her position, to regroup, to reconsider options… to make a new plan. If you are ready to put yourself back in control and to refocus your direction, you are ready to take charge…ready to make a plan. *THIS plan is guaranteed*!

Start by sitting down, taking a few minutes (and a deep breath), and drawing yourself a MAP (a PLAN). Believe it or not, the toughest part is to establish: **"What do I WANT?"**

Take your time and *really* think it through. Then begin mapping it out — *literally writing it out* — HOW you intend to get there. There are only four simple questions to answer for each goal, so give it a try.

1. WHAT do I *really* WANT?   (Goal #___)
2. WHAT am I currently DOING about getting this thing I WANT?
3. Is what I'm doing now, working for me to get this thing I WANT?
4. No? Then I'll make a PLAN (step by step) to get this thing I want?
(Note: If it takes more than 3-5 Steps, then your Goal (your WANT) is too broad.)

If you have been "LOST" for some time, you may have to refer to this MAP every day for a while. You can make appropriate course changes along the way, but the GOAL… that which you said you *really* wanted… remains the focus. Adjust your plan when necessary by acknowledging when steps are completed, and when difficult steps need more of your attention.

If you focus your attention on completing EACH step, you will not only reach your goal, there is no way you cannot!

When enough is enough!

You know that the longer a break in a relationship remains, the harder it will be for that relationship to heal. You try to pretend that being IN conflict doesn't bother you. In fact, you've tried to ignore it, but you can't shake it. Unresolved thoughts and feelings will be taken inside… and harbored. The longer they are there, the more painful it becomes. Without acting on those thoughts and feelings, it won't let go.

This conflict of yours has been allowed to persist for a long time, hasn't it? You've tried, but it refuses to be ignored, it can't be avoided, and it won't be denied its power to consume your thoughts and disturb your sleep. Until you DO something about what you're thinking, the knot in you stomach will always be there to remind you.

Have you tried to admit you were wrong, accept a failing, finally forgiven yourself (or another), or faced the person you have allowed to consume your thoughts? If not, you have taken that which has been troubling you and granted it authority over your mind and body. You have given yourself permission for this *thing* to take over your life.

Your inaction has allowed this *thing* to fester within you. It has…or it soon will… begin its travels from prolonged mental anguish, through a never ending roller coaster of emotions, to the physical pain that you'll come to accept as headaches, nausea, back pain and more severe physical distress.

Haven't you had enough? Are you ready to face your demon? Ask yourself: *Is this thing that is bothering me so horrible that facing it could be worse than I'm feeling right now?*

The only way past conflict is through it.
And the longer you delay, the more painful the journey.

Anger BEGINS from WITHIN

We create our own anger. Outside stimuli can only stir what is already there. The experiences, perceptions, and understanding people have within them will "allow" a comment or action to positively or negatively influence their judgments and actions. We can't control what others say or do, and sometimes that "makes us angry." How dare others not have the same feelings, insecurities, or experiences as we do? When others stubbornly refuse to be controlled by us, or they don't see life the way we do, we get "angry" with them and say, *"YOU made me angry."*

Sometimes we could just kick ourselves for the things we say or do—or what we have *failed* to say or do. We mere mortals often have the inability to accept that we could have misspoken, said something inappropriate, out-of-line, or just stupid! We don't always allow ourselves to recover from our own lapses in judgment, to make a mistake, or to be seen as less than perfect. We fear others may think less of us (loss of Acceptance), they will restrict our independence (lack of Freedom), or ridicule our errors, and make folly out of our sincerity (lack of Importance or Fulfillment). We become defensive when we are challenged. We repress an apology and scream when we should have laughed, experience guilt for any one of a number of exposed imperfections, and are quick to point the finger of blame at others. Anger is not the fault of others. Our inability to accept our own failings is the source of our anger.

When left unresolved, anger turns inward. Doctors first call that stress. When left to manifest, they will later call that depression.

YOU choose what seeds to plant.

Once upon a time, there were two farmers. Each farmer had a field. Each field had an equal amount of nutrients, nitrogen, and other elements necessary for the production of healthy crops. Each fertile field received the same amount of sunshine and water. In one field, seeds of corn were planted: an edible and nutritious crop. In the other: seeds of nightshade, which is a deadly poison. As each field received an equal amount of tending, water, and sunshine, each crop grew to a bountiful harvest: one with corn, the other with poison.

The human mind is exactly like that...what you plant will grow. If you plant positive seeds, only positive seeds will take over your garden. If you plant poison, you need not be surprised that only negativity and doubt will consume your thoughts. Whatever YOU plant, will grow, for there will be no room for anything else.

Only YOU can be responsible for YOU. Only you can choose your behaviors. Only you can choose to remain in an emotional well — the well cannot choose you. You can choose to serve only you, or you can choose behaviors that will serve others; behaviors that will also reward you!

What you sow. . .you shall also reap.

The Pygmalion Effect

As you learn from your experiences, you determine for yourself what is right and wrong (for yourself). The more experiences you develop, the more you see yourself as the model of "*nearly perfect*" (for others). Consequently, since you know what nearly perfect looks like, you expect everyone else to be "nearly perfect," too (defining "nearly perfect" to mean that *they* are doing what *you* think *they* should be doing).

Now brace yourself. Everyone else believes they are "nearly perfect" too. There is actually a name for this: It is called the Pygmalion Effect. When you are not "nearly perfect" by the standards of others, others take it upon themselves to point this out to you. They are as quick to point out your imperfections…as you are to correct others when they are not living up to your *standards*. It is as if each persons' purpose on the planet is to make sure the *other* guy knows each and every time he fails to measure up. After all, when *you* make a mistake, misspell a word, show poor judgment, display bad etiquette, have lousy manners, have a bad hair day, wear clothing in poor taste, mispronounce a word, display a lack of driving skills, etc., isn't there *always* somebody right there to point it out to you?

**Maybe this explains why the lady holding the Scales of Justice
is wearing a blindfold: We judge ourselves by our intentions…
but we judge others by their actions.**

TAKE the RISK

Think of a time when you received a warm and generous smile from a stranger, heard a rather moving message from your pastor, enjoyed an exceptional dinner, or received a tender hug from a child. Using any one of a thousand such examples, how often did you acknowledge the impact that moment had on you? You thought about it, but you just couldn't seem to say it out loud.

If you never spoke the first word about it to the person who had this positive impact on you, how would he or she truly know that such simple expressions of love, recognition, or gratitude meant so much to you?

While it does take two to make a relationship, it all begins with *YOU* placing the focus on *others*. Our ability to build positive relationships is dependent upon our willingness to reach out to others and to care about what *others* care about.

Unfair? You want people to come to you first? You want to sit back and wait for someone to include you? You want others to notice you and then you'll feel welcomed and ready to join in? Well, brace yourself because that is exactly how *other* people see it, too! If you want to be included, invited, encouraged, and welcomed, then it's all about *you* taking the first step. Be the first to smile, offer a greeting, open a door, shake a hand, or offer a cup of coffee. These are painless attempts that will meet the needs of others. It may literally open a dialogue that may never have had a chance if you did not first extend the invitation.

This is why the people out front are called LEADERS.

Understanding
precedes ACCEPTANCE

- Do you understand that conflict, though unwelcome, comes from within, is natural, and will remain a constant companion?

- Do you understand that what you meant is not always what others will hear?

- Do you understand that you can't fix another person? Although you may be well-intentioned and have a desire to be supportive or "helpful," keep in mind that others don't see themselves as broken*!*

- Do you understand that you have the power to shut down the life-draining gossip that whirls around you, and that you can do it in a single sentence?

- Do you understand that when exposed to gossip and rumor the very next words that come from you may set you apart from Interpersonal conflict, or place you in the center of it?

We are ALL one body.

Line Leadership is a collegial leadership model. It is a principle that recognizes the value each employee brings into the organization. It accepts the premise behind this fundamental statement, *"There are many parts… but we are all one body."*

Leaders with this philosophy do not label their employees on a traditional pyramid leadership chart with the bosses on the top and the others ranked in various steps below. Line Leadership says, *"I am on this line somewhere and you are on this line somewhere. I can't do my job without you, and you can not do your job without me and the rest of us on this line. Our differences are our gifts to each other and to those this organization serves."*

Everyone must bring their own unique gifts and talents to the table. In this, we ALL succeed.

Summary

You want a better life? You want better relationships with those around you? You want people to like you, to respect you, and to include you in their lives? You want to stop hoping for it… and begin realizing it? Then it is… as it has always been… ***all about you*** to make that happen. Life is NOT a dress rehearsal… so begin NOW.

If you choose to do something different than yesterday, that choice belongs to YOU... and you alone. Even the decision *not* to decide is yours. To believe you "have to" stick with 'the way we've always done it,' remain in a job you hate, stay in a repressive relationship, withhold a compliment, ask for a raise, or eat that last donut, these are all…like leadership itself… decisions that you must make for yourself. You have only to give yourself permission.

Your desire to find happiness, more appropriate relationships, a better job, or to do whatever you intrinsically know will be better decisions for the people you serve… is as close as the very next decision that you make. It has not been your *destiny* that has led you to this point in your life but your *decisions*. Not happy with the habits that have taken you here? Then make a plan, abandon your habits, and take the first step in a direction that only YOU must choose.

Peace,

IN THE 21ST CENTURY—IT IS STILL—
ALL ABOUT THE CULTURE

Tod Faller Presents:

Four Dynamic Interpersonal Communication Seminars from The Teacher Down the Hall Seminar Series

Goal of the Seminars: Leaders of 21st Century Professional Learning Communities will demonstrate and inspire a culture for understanding, accepting and resolving Interpersonal Conflict.

Objective of the Seminars: To Build Professional Learning *Comm-unities,* Leaders must inspire *Common-Unity* among the Learners.

Outcome of the Seminars: Participants will acknowledge personal accountability for the formation of positive relationships and work teams within a community of learners... Guaranteed.

Workshops

1 "What did you do THAT for?"

Recognize the difference between our human NEEDS and our human BEHAVIORS. You can't be expected to understand every human behavior...but you CAN easily understand these five basic Needs: the motivation behind every behavior. Be willing to look behind the negative or inappropriate behaviors of others, to help OTHERS meet THEIR Needs, and *THEY* will go out of their way to meet *YOUR* Needs...*Guaranteed!*

2 "Excuse me? Did you just say what I thought I saw?"

Personal and professional relationships are dependent upon understanding OTHERS and how others are to understand US. A thousand times a day we speak through our Words, Inflection, and Body Language (non-verbals). Hear what others are really saying to you...even when they're saying nothing at all.

3 "You taught me to READ, now teach me to LISTEN."

True communications and understanding is *never* in the intent of the speaker; it is *always* in the message received by the listener. We humans NEED to *relate* to each other. Relationships will be built and conflicts resolved when you practice these four "A's" of Active Listening. You will be amazed how *OTHERS* will begin treating *YOU* differently, more positively, and *THEY* won't even know why they're doing it...*Guaranteed!*

4 Can't we all just get along?

The answer of course, is YES: but not all at the same time. Our human BEHAVIORS separate us, our basic NEEDS unite us, but it is our PERSONALITY that provides the balance. In this active, fun and highly charged hands-on seminar, participants will learn their own personality traits, and the traits of those around them. Participants will immediately discover why some people excel in certain tasks, yet flounder in others. And the question will be answered as to why you choose to admire and respect some folks...yet remain in conflict with others.

The Teacher Down the Hall Seminar Series

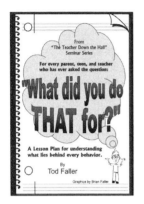